Dinnee

The Li

CW00665963

Dinneen and the Dictionary:
The Life and the Afterlife
Pádraigín Riggs

Occasional Lecture Series 5
First Published by the Irish Texts Society
2021
© Copyright Irish Texts Society
www.irishtextssociety.org

ISBN: 978-1-9998047-9-4

The Irish Texts Society
c/o Royal Bank of Scotland
Drummonds Branch
49 Charing Cross
Admiralty Arch
London SW1A 2DX

Dinneen and the Dictionary:
The Life and the Afterlife

Pádraigín Riggs

Irish Texts Society

Cumann na Scríbheann nGaedhilge

Occasional Lecture Series 5

London, 2021

Dinneen and the Dictionary: The Life and the Afterlife

Part 1: The Life
Dinneen's Biography

An Duinníneach, first published in 1958, by Sáirséal agus Dill and co-authored by Proinsias Ó Conluain, from Sessia-magaroll, Clonfeacle, Co. Tyrone and Donncha Ó Céileachair, from Cúil Aodha in the West Cork Gaeltacht, is the only attempt, to date, at writing a full biography of Pádraig Ua Duinnín.[1] In an article he contributed to volume five of *Scríobh* in 1981, Ó Conluain describes how the book came about and how he and Ó Céileachair collaborated in its writing.[2] Initially conceived in 1952 as a radio series, 'Fear agus Foclóir' was based on scripts submitted to Ó Conluain, who worked for Radio Éireann, by various persons who knew Fr Dinneen.[3] After the programmes were broadcast, the scripts were put aside and it was not until 1955, when Ernest Blythe suggested that Dinneen would make a suitable subject for a biography, that Ó Conluain commenced adapting the scripts as material for a book. In addition to the radio scripts, he used material from Dinneen's published work — books, pamphlets and articles in journals and newspapers as well as the letters and manuscripts attributed to him in the National Library. When he mentioned to Donncha Ó Céileachair, at a meeting of Cumann na Scríbhneoirí, that the demands of his work as a radio documentary maker were preventing him from making progress with the Dinneen biography, Ó Céileachair, who was working with Tomás de Bhaldraithe on the English-Irish

---

[1] *An Duinníneach* has not been translated to English and has been out of print for some years.

[2] 'An Duinníneach — Comhar Liteartha', in S. Ó Mórdha (eag.), *Scríobh* 5 (Baile Átha Cliath, 1981) 182–90.

[3] These persons included An tAthair Donnchadh Ó Floinn, Seosamh Ó Muirthile S.J., Fiachra Éilgeach (Risteard Ó Foghludha), Piaras Béaslaí, Nuala Ní Mhóráin, Aindrias Ó Muimhneacháin, Pádraig Ó Conchubhair from the National Library and others. L.S. Gogan, one of Dinneen's main assistants in the Dictionary project, contributed a substantial account but withdrew it when he learned that Risteard Ó Foghludha was also a participant.

1

Dictionary at that time, offered to assist him. And so the collaboration began.

The pair soon realised that they had material, not for one book on Pádraig Ua Duinnín, but for four, covering four separate aspects of his life and work. However, they edited the material to produce a single volume, summarising it as follows: 'There were at least four different Dinneens in the course of the seventy odd years he lived — the Kerryman in Sliabh Luachra (twenty years a-growing), the Jesuit (twenty years in shelter), the Gaelic Leaguer, the lone bird and many others that would be difficult to categorise. It is all of these different, elusive Dinneens, as well as the literary and the scholarly Dinneen, that we shall attempt to discuss in the following pages'.[4] Having decided on early 1956 as a deadline, with the intention of entering the book for a competition in that year's Oireachtas, the two authors — one from Ulster, the other from Munster — agreed to reject their respective dialects in favour of a version of Irish that would be comprehensible to all speakers of the language. This was a major challenge, which necessitated more editing and rewriting than had been originally anticipated. The standardisation of the language, resulting in the publication in 1958 of *Caighdeán Oifigiúil na Gaeilge*, was a controversial issue at that time but Ó Conluain and Ó Céileachair, together with their chosen publisher, Seán Ó hÉigeartaigh, all had very considerable expertise in the use of Standard Irish. The result of the collaboration was an award-winning publication which remains one of the most outstanding examples of Modern Irish prose, derived from an expert knowledge of the spoken language yet, highly literary, free from awkward neologisms and stylistically elegant.

---

[4] 'Bhí ceathrar Duinníneach éagsúla ar a laghad ann sa bhreis is seachtó bliain dar mhair sé — An Ciarraíoch i Sliabh Luachra (fiche bliain ag fás), an t-Íosánach (fiche bliain faoi scáth), an Conrathóir, an cadhan aonraic agus go leor eile a mbeadh sé deacair aon lipéad aitheantais ar leith a chur leo. Is iad na Duinnínigh éagsúla éalaitheacha sin, maraon le Duinnínigh na litríochta agus na scoláireachta, a bhfuil sé d'aidhm againne plé leo sna leathanaigh atá le teacht': Ó Conluain agus Ó Céileachair, *An Duinníneach*, 25 (translations from Irish are mine, unless otherwise stated).

Drawing on the four aspects of the subject's life referred to above, the biography comprises a total of six sections. A list of Dinneen's miscellaneous writings, published and unpublished, is appended along with a bibliography of the written sources consulted. The first section presents a portrait of Dinneen, the eccentric public figure, described by the authors as 'one of Dublin's characters'. Section II (1860–80), which deals with his background in the Sliabh Luachra region, is an outstanding depiction of life in the nineteenth century in an area renowned for its rich literary culture. Ó Céileachair had a special competence when dealing with this subject; as a native of Cúil Aodha, he had an intimate personal knowledge of the region and its people and he also had an academic knowledge of its topography and onomastics.[5] Dinneen's early education is outlined in this section, first, at the school where his uncle, Mícheál Ó Donnchadha ('Mick the Master') was the teacher and later, in Rathmore, where he received lessons in Latin from Father Conchubhar Ó Súilleabháin. It was Father Ó Súilleabháin who introduced him to Father Donncha Ó Murchú S.J., when the latter was visiting the locality, and the two priests were instrumental in Dinneen's decision to enter the Jesuit order.

The section on the Jesuit years (1880–1900) describes the strict regulations which aspirants to the Society of Jesus had to observe and the formation that Dinneen had to undergo both in the Novitiate and as a university undergraduate. It was while he was a member of the Jesuits that he began to take an interest in Irish, even though he had been exposed to the language from childhood. It seems that one of those who encouraged this interest was Father John MacErlean whom he got to know when both priests were teaching in Clongowes Wood College; Dinneen taught English, Mathematics and Physics at the school. Dinneen was later reticent about this period of his life, and the reasons for his departure from the Jesuits after twenty years are not explained, though his obstinate personality seems to have been a significant factor.

---

[5] He had been contemplating doing a doctoral thesis on the place names of Sliabh Luachra for which he had collected a substantial amount of material.

The section on the Gaelic League (1900–09) documents the activities of that organisation during one of the most important periods in its history. Dinneen, a member and for a time, President, of the Keating Branch played a prominent role in the League, participating in all of its major committees, and assuming a controversial standpoint on the foremost issues in which it was engaged, notably those concerned with education and publication. His relations with many of the prominent individuals in the Language Movement were difficult and, in some cases, extremely acrimonious. He severed his connection with the Gaelic League in 1909, following the controversy over the question of compulsory Irish in the National University.

The fifth section (1910–34) covers the difficult years during which he was struggling with the challenging project that was the second edition of the Dictionary, up to his death in 1934. We are given little insight into that personal struggle, however, as the account consists mainly of reminiscences of Dinneen by friends and acquaintances.

The final section, 'His Literary Work' ('A Shaothar Liteartha'), as well as discussing Dinneen's considerable labour as a literary editor, contains a lengthy discussion of the Dictionaries, particularly the 1927 edition, and includes a brief account of the dispute with Fr O'Hickey. Reference is made to reviews of the Dictionary, both favourable and critical, and many of the work's flaws and idiocycracies are identified and analysed, reflecting Ó Céileachair's native expertise as well as that acquired while working on the de Bhaldraithe dictionary. However, the concluding assessment is overwhelmingly positive, describing the work as being regarded 'more as a Bible than a dictionary by Irish speakers'.[6]

Much of the evidence on which the biography depends is contextual or anecdotal which is understandable considering the nature of the sources already referred to, and statements are frequently hedged, with the result that the Dinneen who emerges is predominantly one perceived by others, while personal revelations are largely absent;

---

[6] 'Is mó de Bhíobla ná de fhoclóir ag Gaeilgeoirí é'.

4

consequently, the private person remains elusive. He is described by the authors on more than one occasion as being reticent or unforthcoming about certain aspects of his life:

> You could say that his contemporaries knew Dinneen well but they would admit that it was difficult to know him fully. He was always somewhat mysterious — [there were] certain areas of his life and certain deep caverns in his mind that he was unwilling to reveal to anyone. Even Muiris Ó Droighneáin, while compiling *Taighde i gcomhair Stair Litríochta na Nua-Ghaeilge*, failed to extract any biographical notes from him, even though they both sat beside each other every day in the National Library.[7]

The section on his youth in Sliabh Luachra, as already mentioned, provides an excellent depiction of the people and the region, but the authors admit that they 'know very little about Pádraig Ó Duinnín's childhood. He was always very unforthcoming with information about that period of his life or about anything connected with his people, his native place or anything private'.[8] While such reticence may appear odd, Ó Conluain and Ó Céileachair simply attribute it to a certain rural mentality rather than to any personal reason on Dinneen's part. At other times, they resort to speculation, most notably when dealing with his period as a Jesuit:

---

[7] 'D'fhéadfá a rá go raibh aithne mhaith ag na daoine sin uile a bhí comhaimserach leis ar an Athair Ó Duinnin ach d'admhóidís féin gur dheacair aithne iomlán a chur air. Bhí rúndiamhracht éigin ag baint leis i gcónaí — ranna airithe dá shaol agus uamhacha áirithe dá intinn nár thoiligh sé a nochtadh d'aoinne. Fiú amháin Muiris Ó Droighneáin, le linn dó bheith ag cur *Taighde i gcomhair Stair Litríochta na Nua-Ghaeilge* le chéile, ní fhéadfadh sé aon nótaí beathaisnéise a fháil uaidh, cé go mbíodh an bheirt acu ina suí in aice a chéile gach lá sa Leabharlann Náisiunta': Ó Conluain and Ó Céileachair, *An Duinníneach*, 24.

[8] 'Ní heol dúinn mórán fá óige Phádraig Uí Dhuinnín. Bhí sé an-choigilteach é féin i gcónaí maidir le heolas a thabhairt fán tréimhse sin dá shaol nó fá aon ní a bhain lena mhuintir, lena áit dúchais nó le cúrsaí príobhaideacha d'aon sórt': ibid., 61.

We do not know what spiritual problems he grappled with in the Jesuits or what effect the intellect of Ignatius Loyola had on him — apart, perhaps, from some minor personal traits which became manifest later and which could have been connected to that hidden regulated period of his life.[9]

Following the account of the conflict with Father O'Hickey, we are told: '... it would be fruitless on our part to assign any logic or any certainty in terms of action or attitude to Dinneen in any matters at all. He was unfathomable, inscrutable always'.[10] However, one place where Dinneen revealed his personality, although still not in an intimite or comprehensive way, was the Dictionary. 'Anyone who knew him, said his colleague, Father Donnchadh Ó Floinn, will see on every page of the dictionary some word, or some expression, or a piece of information, or some wordplay that will bring Father Pádraig back to life for him'.[11] It may be the case that the Dictionary was the place where Dinneen came closest to revealing himself, albeit in a limited and indirect way. In the much-quoted phrase: 'He and his dictionary were one and the same, and together they were tantamount to a national institution'.[12]

When they were writing their biography, Ó Conluain and Ó Céileachair did not have access to important documents that would have provided them with information on the tortuous history of the first edition of the Dictionary, from its inception to its publication in 1904, or on the many difficulties

---

[9] 'Ní heol dúinn cad iad na fadhbanna spioradálta a ndearna sé coraíocht leo i gCumann Íosa ná cad é an tionchar a bhí ag intleacht Loyola air — amach ó thréithe beaga pearsanta, b'fhéidir, a nocht iad féin nios déanaí agus a bhféadfadh baint a bheith acu leis an ré rialta folaithe sin dá shaol': ibid., 80.

[10] '... ba neamhthairbheach an mhaise dúinn aon chéim loighiciúil nó aon chinnteacht ghníomhaíochta nó dearctha a chur síos don Duinnineach in aon chúrsaí ar leith. Bhí sé dobhraite, dothomhaiste i gcónaí': ibid., 225.

[11] 'Aon duine a raibh aithne aige air, adúirt a chomhoibrí, an tAthair Donnchadh Ó Floinn, chífidh sé ar gach aon leathanach den fhoclóir focal éigin, nó nathán éigin, nó blúire eolais éigin, nó focailín éigin imeartais a chuirfeas an tAthair Pádraig thar n-ais ar an saol chuige': ibid., 343.

[12] 'Ba aoinne amháin é féin agus a fhoclóir, agus ba gheall le hinstitiúid náisiúnta iad araon': ibid., 341.

associated with the completion of the second, enlarged, edition in 1927. These documents, the Minute Books and Correspondence of the Irish Texts Society, had been held by that Society in their archives in London until 1994.[13] When these archives became available for consultation, it was possible to provide a more detailed account of the tribulations and triumphs experienced both by the compiler of the Dictionary and by his publisher.[14] The correspondence they contain provides an enhanced insight into Dinneen, the person.

In 2004, to mark the centenary of the publication of the first edition of The Dictionary, the Irish Texts Society devoted their Annual Seminar to the life and work of Dinneen.[15] Contributions included papers which gave an updated perspective on aspects of the Ó Conluain and Ó Céileachair narrative, including Dinneen's involvement with the Gaelic League, his acquaintance with the song tradition of Sliabh Luachra and an extensive account of his contention with Fr O'Hickey as well as a comprehensive analysis of his lexicological legacy.

In 2013, University College Dublin Press published a long essay entitled *The Queen of the Hearth*, by Patrick S. Dinneen, edited from a manuscript in the National Library of Ireland by Philip O'Leary who also provides an Introduction to the work. According to O'Leary, 'internal evidence makes it obvious that the work was written during World War 1, though it is difficult to say precisely when'.[16] Written in English, this book deals with the role of women in the domestic and public

---

13 See P. Ó Riain, 'Archives of the Society', in idem (ed.), *Irish Texts Society: The First Hundred Years*, Irish Texts Society, Subsidiary Series 9 (Dublin, 1998) 75–103 at 75.

14 See P. Riggs, 'The Beginnings of the Society', in Ó Riain (ed.), *Irish Texts Society: The First Hundred Years*, 2–35. See, eadem, 'An Duinníneach: Aguisín', in J. Carey, M. Herbert and K. Murray (eds), *Cín Chille Cúile: Texts, Saints and Places—Essays in Honour of Pádraig Ó Riain*, Celtic Studies Publications 9 (Aberystwyth, 2004) 367–80.

15 The proceedings of this event were later published as P. Riggs (ed.), *Dinneen and the Dictionary: 1904–2004*, Irish Texts Society, Subsidiary Series 16 (London, 2005).

16 P.S. Dinneen, *Queen of the Hearth*, with an introduction by P. O'Leary, Classics of Irish History (Dublin, 2013) p. xxii.

sphere at a time when that role was undergoing radical changes.[17] The tenor of the essay can be summarised in the following statement:

> The hearth is their [women's] sphere of life, the theatre of their joys and triumphs. Nature has planted in their souls an instinct which never gets its full satisfaction outside the sacred precincts of home life … The hearth, then, is the centre of happiness, the life, the activity of womankind. She fills a position which women in general are instinctively aiming at as a crowning happiness.[18]

This book reflects a side of Dinneen that has no obvious connection to the lexicographer and language activist; indeed, as O'Leary says, in this work 'he eliminated everything that might identify him not only as an Irish-language activist, but even as Irish at all'.[19] When his biographers admitted that there were Dinneens that 'would be difficult to categorise', they might well have imagined the author of *Queen of the Hearth*. However, they were either unaware of the contents of this essay, or did not consider it relevant to their story. They list the folder in the National Library Manuscript Collection which contains the manuscript on which the book is based, but they simply provide a general description of its contents: '8623: 24 folders. Literary remnants in English — essays on politics, nationalism, education, religion, etc. Verses, stories, etc.'.[20]

---

[17] Dinneen had, of course, been an active columnist for almost twenty-five years, writing for D.P. Moran's paper, *The Leader*, but *The Queen of the Hearth* was not part of his contribution to that paper.

[18] Ibid., 13–14.

[19] Ibid., p. xxii.

[20] '24 fillteáin. Iarsmaí liteartha i mBéarla — aistí ar chúrsaí polaitíochta, náisiúnachais, oideachais, creidimh, etc. Véarsaí, scéalta, etc.': Ó Conluain and Ó Céileachair, *An Duinníneach*, 362.

Part 2: The Afterlife
The Dictionary

The second edition of Dinneen's Dictionary, 'An Foclóir Mór', was published by the Irish Texts Society in 1927, twenty-three years after the publication of the first edition. A reprint of the 1904 Dictionary had been mooted as early as 1915 though without any sense of urgency, as 400 copies were still available. However, when the plates were destroyed by a fire at the printers during the 1916 Rising, only seven copies were left and in March 1917, the Council of the Society approached Dinneen to ask for his opinion regarding a new edition. In his reply, he proposed that 'the additional material should be such an amount as to make the book new and distinctive and up to date and satisfy reasonably the dialect wants'.[21] Following lengthy negotiations, which generated a substantial amount of correspondence, a contract between Pádraig Ua Duinnín and the Council of the Irish Texts Society was signed on 1.9.1919.[22] According to the terms of the contract: 'The editor agrees to prepare peruse correct alter edit and superintend through the press a complete and perfect alphabetical Dictionary known as the larger Irish-English Dictionary within a period of about four years from the date hereof'.[23] The completion of the project actually took twice that length of time.

Summarising the contents of the Society's Minute Books for the period 31.1.1925 to 26.1.1929, Pádraig Ó Riain says:

> It was [T.D.] Fitzgerald's great achievement to have seen Dinneen's Dictionary successfully through the press. Despite enormous difficulties encountered along the way, many of which were created by the editor, the Dictionary was finally published late in the year 1927 and, at a Council meeting on 28.1.1928, one of two specially bound and interleaved copies of

---

[21] ITS Archives, Box 14 (quoted in Riggs, 'An Duinníneach: Aguisín', 369).
[22] See Riggs, 'An Duinníneach: Aguisín', 380.
[23] ITS Archives, Box 14.

the work was proudly placed on the table by
Fitzgerald.[24]

Ó Riain adds, in a footnote: 'There is now no trace of this
copy'. There is no mention of the second of the 'two specially
bound and interleaved' dictionaries. In the Minutes of the
Council meeting (13th December 1927) an item headed
'Dictionary: Special binding and interleaved copies' mentions
a letter from a Mr Lyon 'asking for 50 copies in sheets for one
or two interleaved copies and for having one or two bound in
leather … Interleaved copies in two volumes in buckram
would cost 25/– for the two'.[25] There is no explanation for the
interleaving — whether, for example, it was intended to garner
new material for an amended or expanded edition of the newly
published volume. When the first edition was published,
twelve interleaved copies were also ordered.[26] A typed
document (item xvi), marked 'strictly private' states that:

> In view of ultimately issuing a completely revised
> edition (…) prizes (…) have been offered by the
> Council for (…) lists of words not contained in the
> present volume. The date for sending in the lists has
> been extended from March 31st to May 1st 1907 and
> there is (…) a prospect that useful lists will be (…)
> submitted for competition.[27]

In the Editor's Preface to the 1927 edition, the lists that
resulted from this competition are acknowledged: 'Use has
also been made of some of the lists obtained in the prize
competition instituted by the Council of the Irish Texts Society
some years ago'.[28]

---

[24] Ó Riain, 'Archives of the Society', 85. T.D. Fitzgerald was Joint Honorary
Secretary of the Society until August 1928.
[25] ITS Archives, Box 3.
[26] See ITS Minutes, 27 September 1904 (ITS Archives, Box 1).
[27] ITS Archives, Box 1.
[28] *Foclóir Gaedhilge agus Béarla: An Irish-English Doctionary*, compiled and
edited by Rev. Patrick S. Dinneen, M.A., Irish Texts Society (Dublin, 1927) p.
xiv.

The question of a Supplement to the 1927 edition did arise, however, seven years after its publication. In April 1934, following an agreement made at the previous AGM of the Society, a reprint was ordered 'with additions and corrections and 300 new words supplied by Father Dinneen'.[29] Dinneen had wished to include another list of words but Dr Robin Flower considered that 'this, and any further lists of words should be kept for a possible Supplement to the Dictionary'.[30] The Minutes then state: 'The Council decided, in view of certain correspondence in the Press, that Fr. Dinneen's views on the publication of the Supplement should be obtained and that he should be asked to collect his lists of words with that end in view'.[31]

In a letter dated 4.6.1934, Dinneen wrote to the Secretary of the Society:

> I assume that there is no question of a revision of the book at present.
>
> A Supplement should embrace the most necessary and characteristic words etc. not to be found in the book. Those words etc. would be culled from the material which has appeared in print since the book was published and as far as possible from a study of the living dialects of the three provinces ...
>
> The preparation of such a Supplement is obviously a slow and tedious process. Lists of words are generally of little value unless compiled by persons with a competent knowledge of the language spoken and written and of the Dictionary. Even in the case of the latter a careful sifting would be necessary.[32]

On September 29th, Dinneen died. A month later, on 27th October, L.S. Gogan wrote to the Secretary:

---

[29] Minutes of Council, 24 April, 1934: ITS Archives, Box 3.
[30] Ibid.
[31] Ibid.
[32] ITS Archives, Box 16.

11

Now that Dr. Dinneen is dead, you will probably be requiring a continuator. I might be prepared to take this on. As you know, I carried out the complete final revision from the end of the letter 'A' on, and reduced the miscellaneous stuff to something like a system, adding of course, a tremenduous amount of new material. So radical was my work that he asked your Society to link my name with his in the edition but somehow your members were not very sympathetic towards me at the time and apparently took steps to prevent this.[33]

O'Connell replied, with apologies for the delay, on 3 February 1935:

I think I mentioned to you in one of my letters that we had been discussing the question of a Supplement to the Dictionary. So far, this has gone no further except to get Fr. Dinneen's views on what a Supplement would be like, etc. It was suggested at the meeting, however, that I should ask you to state your views more fully especially with reference to the question of editorship.[34]

On February 6th, Gogan replied, saying:

I am interested in what you say about a supplement to the Dictionary and the considerations concerning the editorship.

You ask me to state my views in regard to the latter but I must confess I cannot see clearly the scope of your question. Does it refer to our previous correspondence or is there a proposal that I should resume the editorship?

O'Connell has pencilled a note of the back of this letter saying:

---

[33] Ibid.
[34] Ibid.

There is nothing decided about the Supplement yet, in fact no definite proposals so far, it is still 'in the air' one might say. But your letter served to draw more definite attention to it.[35]

On March 8th 1935, Maurice O'Connell wrote to Tomás Ó Deirg, then Minister for Education:

> A chara,
> The Council of this Society have under consideration the question of a supplement to the Society's Larger Irish-English Dictionary, edited by the late Rev. P.S. Dinneen. We are anxious to learn the extent of the demand for such a supplement and to obtain first-hand information as to the necessity for publishing it. In deciding these points, among others, it would be necessary to take into consideration words not already in the Dictionary and the desirability, or otherwise, of including new words. We shall be glad to have your opinion, as Minister of Education, on this matter, and on any other points that may occur to you in connection with the suggested supplement.[36]

Copies of this letter were sent to Dr O. Bergin, Professor T.F. O'Rahilly and Dr Myles Dillon. On May 7th, Myles Dillon replied:

> A chara,
> It is not easy to give a satisfactory answer to your letter without having seen the work in question. There is no doubt about the demand for such a supplement. I feel sure that, if it is published at a reasonable price, the demand will be immediate, for the pressure in Irish here is now greater than ever. The inclusion of new words, i.e. words invented by officials in the last

[35] Ibid.
[36] Ibid.

few years would be a doubtful service. They should certainly be marked with an asterisk, or otherwise, if included. But this is a matter for the editor. I presume that you will ask some competent person to see Fr Dinneen's work through the press. In case you come to consider the matter, the following names of competent persons occur to me:

Professor O'Donoghue of Cork

Professor Tomás Ó Máille

Dr M.A. O'Brien, Queen's University, Belfast.

Another sound authority on the modern language is Colm Ó Murchadha, Secretary to Dáil Éireann, but I do not know whether he would have the leisure for the work.[37]

Some months later, the question of a Supplement emerged from another source. On December 13th 1935, Éamon de Valera, addressed the inaugural meeting of the Gaelic Society of the National University at University College Dublin. Risteárd Ó Foghludha ('Fiachra Éilgeach') was present in the audience, and on the following day, he wrote to Maurice O'Connell:

Dear Sir,

At last night's inaugural meeting of the Gaelic Society of the National University, President de Valera, Chancellor of the University, said: 'He would like to see a new edition of the Dinneen Dictionary, which would contain many more specimens of the speech than were contained in the present editions …

A rumour here in Dublin is to the effect that your Society purpose to issue a supplement to the 1927 edition of the Dictionary. In this connection I would say that about 1917 your Society asked if I would kindly place at the disposal of their editor the additions and corrections I had been making during

[37] Ibid. T.F. O'Rahilly considered that the matter should be left until the whole Dictionary could be re-edited.

the previous 13 years, a thing I would have been perfectly willing to do for a reasonable consideration. At the Council's request, I submitted my treble interleaved 1904 edition [in two very bulky volumes] to the late Father Dinneen at the R.I.A. He strongly urged me to hand them over gratis, but to this I demurred — <u>as I am confident he himself would have done in similar circumstances</u> — and the work is still in my possession, <u>unused</u>, and I think it well to remind you of the fact, in case the Council might be disposed to consider the matter of utilising these additions and corrections in the now mooted supplement.[38]

In a second letter, also dated 14 December, 1935, Ó Foghludha says:

> With reference to the matter of the accompanying letter, I would mention that at the moment my services are available for editorial work in Irish, as I am now free from ordinary business responsibilities … Readers of your Dictionaries will have seen my name appearing complimentarily in three places in the 1904 edition [which I read three times before publication] but my name was deliberately omitted from the 1927 edition, notwithstanding that last paragraph on p. xiii, and in spite of the fact that in that edition all the words marked 'B' [Ballymacoda] or 'Condon' [Pádraig Phiarais Cúndún] were supplied by me for the first edition, and virtually all the additions and corrections at the end of the 1904 edition. Over this slight, however, I feel not the slightest resentment, though it annoyed many of my old friends in Dublin.[39]

---

[38] ITS Archives, Box 16 (underlining in the original version). In a letter from Dinneen to the Council of the Society, dated February 1919, he says 'I thought and still think that Mr R. Foley's charge for his list of words was extravagant but it is no isolated case': ITS Archives, Box 14.

[39] ITS Archives, Box 14.

It is not clear from this whether Ó Foghludha was proposing himself as a potential editor of the Supplement or for other editorial work. He does not seem to have been a candidate for the post of editor, however.

Little progress seems to have been made on the matter of the Supplement or its editor by August of that year. An unsigned note written by Maurice O'Connell, the Secretary, and dated 25.8.36 states:

> The Council have not yet taken any definite steps towards the issue of the suggested Supplement to the Society's Larger Irish-English Dictionary edited by P.S. Dinneen. At present we are making enquiries as to the whereabouts of certain lists of words that were received too late to be used in the main work but may be useful for the compilation of a Supplement. We hope to receive details of these before long and may then be in a position to do something.[40]

These enquiries continued up to 1939, then the War intervened and the matter was not actively pursued again until 1946 apart from a reference in the Council Minutes for February 8th 1941: 'The desirability of obtaining lists of words not contained in the Dictionary with a view to a possible Supplement was discussed. The Secretary was instructed to write to various university professors and others who were in a position to collect and ask them to do so'.[41]

An Agreement to produce the Supplement was finally made between L.S. Gogan and the Irish Texts Society in 1951.[42] The appointment of Gogan would undoubtedly have pleased Dinneen whose acknowledgement of the latter's contribution to the 1927 edition of the Dictionary was fulsomely expressed

---

[40] ITS Archives, Box 16.

[41] ITS Archives, Box 3.

[42] Fr Lambert McKenna declined the editorship and Tomás de Bhaldraithe, having initially shown an interest, also declined an invitation to edit the Supplement. For an account of the proposed supplement and the related correspondence contained in the Dinneen Files in the Society's Archives, see Ó Riain, 'Archives of the Society', 100–101.

in his Editor's Preface.[43] However, following difficulties between the Society and their appointee, it was decided in 1955 not to proceed with the project and the proposed Supplement never materialised.[44] In 1958, the Department of Education appointed Niall Ó Dónaill to edit a new Irish-English Dictionary for use in schools and by the general public, Dinneen's Dictionary now being considered out of date for such purposes.

In his reference to the two interleaved copies of the Dictionary, one of which T.D. Fitzgerald placed on the table at the Council meeting of the Irish Texts Society in 1928, Pádraig Ó Riain may have been mistaken in his understanding that 'there is now no trace of this [or, of the other] copy'.[45] While it is not possible to say definitively whether or not they are the volumes in question, two interleaved copies of the 1927 edition of Dinneen do exist, each one divided in two and bound, although not in the distinctive binding of the Irish Texts Society — 'buckram binding' had been mentioned when the two interleaved copies were being ordered in December 1927.[46] One pair of half-volumes belonged to Risteárd Ó Foghludha ('Fiachra Éilgeach'), the other, to Seán Óg Ó Caomhánaigh ('Seán a' Chóta).[47] Both are copiously annotated.

Risteárd Ó Foghludha and his Copy of the Dictionary

Risteárd Ó Foghludha was born in 1871, near Killeagh in East Cork, to native Irish-speaking parents. He moved to Dublin in the 1880s where he worked as a journalist, reporting for the *Freeman's Journal*, before moving to England. While there, he sold typewriters for Underwoods and, while still working for that company, moved back to Ireland first to Belfast, then to Dublin, around 1905. He was one of the founding members of the Keating Branch of the Gaelic League to which Dinneen

---

[43] Dinneen, *Foclóir Gaedhilge Béarla*, p. xii.
[44] See Ó Riain, 'Archives of the Society', 101.
[45] Ibid., 85.
[46] Details of circumstances in which these volumes were discovered will be explained in an Afterword.
[47] For his surname, he used both forms: Ó Caomhánaigh and Caomhánach.

17

also belonged, and he collaborated with him on the 1904 edition of the Dictionary. Between 1905 and 1952, he produced editions of fourteen Munster poets as well as publishing translations of plays and stories from French and English. His *Dictionary of Irish Place-names* was published in 1935 and he worked for the Irish Place-names Commission in the 1940s. He received an Honorary D.Litt.Celt. from the National University of Ireland in 1939. Ó Foghludha died in 1957.[48]

Ó Foghludha's copy of the interleaved 1927 Dictionary is divided at the word 'gruthrach' (p. 576). A leaf inserted at the beginning of the first half-volume is dated '20/10/1934' and contains an inscription in Pitman shorthand, giving a brief summary of Dinneen's biography.[49] The date of the inscription is just under one month after Dinneen's death and, coincidentally, one week earlier than the date on Gogan's first letter to the Secretary of the Irish Texts Society offering his services as 'continuator'. On p. xiii of the *Editor's Preface*, the following sentence has been underlined in pencil: 'From the above list no name not given in the list of References has been advertently omitted' and a note was added (in pencil): 'This is an untruth and is deliberate'. As Ó Foghludha remarked in the letter quoted above, his name does not appear in the list but it does occur three times in the Editor's Preface to the 1904 edition (p. xii) which also includes the following acknowledgement: 'Special mention should be made of Mr. Richard Foley's keen interest in the work from the beginning, and of the zeal with which he saught out and recorded local usages'. Relations between the two men had changed radically in the intervening years.[50] The pique that Ó Foghludha felt at

---

[48] D. Breathnach agus M. Ní Mhurchú, *1882–1982: Beathaisnéis a hAon* (Baile Átha Cliath, 1986) 73–4.

[49] I am grateful to Joan McKeating and Kathleen Williamson for decyphering this inscription for me. Ó Foghludha was an expert in shorthand; he was the founder of the Dublin Institute of Shorthand Writers.

[50] One suspicion is that Dinneen resented what he perceived as encroachment on his editorial territory by Ó Foghludha. Both men had been producing editions of the Munster Poets. See Breathnach agus Ní Mhurchú, *1882–1982: Beathaisnéis a hAon*, 74.

having been unfairly omitted from the list of contributors to the 1927 Dictionary was so great that he sought out and highlighted the evidence of the perceived injustice. After the entry '*P.F.* Piaras Mac Gearailt, poems by; ed. Foley, G.L., 1905', 'Foley' is underlined in ink.[51] And '*Condon.* — Patrick Condon, a 19th cent. E. Cork poet' is followed by 'ed. R.Ó Foghludha' also in ink.[52] Ó Foghludha seems to have failed to notice one other reference to his own work, however: '*C.M.* — Cúirt an Mheadhon-Oidhche: editions by Foley and Stern'. In his reappraisal of some of Dinneen's contributions, his bitterness is not concealed.

In his letter to the Irish Texts Society in December 1935, Ó Foghludha refers to 'the additions and notes [he] had been making' between 1904 and 1917, based on the 1904 edition of the Dictionary. It is not possible to say whether or not those notes were subsequently incorporated into the copious additional material included in the 1927 edition. The frequent references to Seán Óg Caomhánach's *Croidhe Cainnte Chiarraighe* — which Ó Foghludha edited between 1935 and 1943 — clearly indicate that he was annotating the Dinneen Dictionary during or after that period. A number of other items contain references that date them from the 1940s. For example, Dinneen does not include the word 'achaill' but Ó Foghludha gives us 'Achaill: cnoc comh-chruinn pointeálta' and his source (apparently) is 'Diarmuid Ó Mathghamhna, Inis Céin 18.4.1945'.[53] 'Adamhach' is not listed by Dinneen either, and Ó Foghludha notes: 'Adamhach: atomic. Búmba a. atomic bomb. 1945'. 'Briosclán' is listed by Dinneen, as 'silver weed, goose-grass, skirret, wild tansey; stunted brittle grass or hay'; Ó Foghludha adds 'Briosclán: corn tansey; palm buttons, etc. *Scéala Éireann* [*The Irish Press*] 12.9.1949'. Beside Dinneen's 'cnag: a knob, a peg; a skein of thread; a hurley-ball'. Ó Foghludha adds 'cnag — bhí an cnag ar bhais a chamáin aige: he had the ball at his foot'. This is followed by what seems to be a name and a date, in Pitman shorthand, and the shorthand

---

[51] Ó Foghludha's interleaved copy, p. xxviii.

[52] Ibid., p. xxiv.

[53] Ibid., p. 4.

19

inscriptions have been glossed in pencil (by another hand?) as 'Fionn Mac Cumhaill' and '23. October 1946'. On the leaf facing p. 707, there is a note in shorthand, followed by the date 23/5/50. Ó Foghludha's revision of the Dictionary seems to have terminated at around that time. His initial offer to the Irish Texts Society, in 1935, was to make his interleaved 1904 edition available to them but it seems that that offer was later updated to include the annotated 1927 edition. On 3.5.1950, he wrote:

> A chaoin-chara,
>
> I duly received your friendly letter. Believe me I appreciate highly the concluding sentence thereof, although I would much prefer that we could have the advantage of another's opinion of the value of my collections. Even now I adopt the plan of saying what I have all along considered a reasonable figure and I leave it to your Council to make me an offer. I own I should much like to see in print the words and phrases of my late parents, grandparents and old neighbours in Imokilly — all of them have passed away 60, 50, 40, 30 years ago, and I would not give a second thought to remuneration, were it not that I am still obliged to be in harness in my 80th year!
>
> The figure I have always had in mind was £50.
>
> I am prepared to assist your editor, whoever he may be, — in any way possible.
>
> I must say here that I was grievously wounded by the final sentence of 'negatives' in the Introduction to the 1927 edition — intended to apply to me alone.
>
> I shall be pleased to hear from you when your Council has come to a decision.
>
> Mise agat,
> Risteárd Ó Foghludha.[54]

[54] ITS Archives, Box 16.

The Society accepted his offer and the two half-volumes were transferred to the Society at the agreed price. A stamped receipt, dated 28 June 1950, was signed by Ó Foghludha:

> Received from the Irish Texts Society the sum of fifty pounds (£50) being full payment for the sale of my two interleaved copies of the Irish Texts Society's dictionaries, published in 1904 and 1927, to the Society for their exclusive use by the Society in connection with the publication of a supplement to its larger dictionary.
>
> Date: 28 June 1950. Signed Risteárd Ó Foghludha.[55]

Ó Foghludha's Notes and Additions — Some Examples

The leaves of Ó Foghludha's 1927 edition do not seem to have been inscribed systematically, that is, by working through the Dictionary once, from beginning to end. On a given page, four different pens may have been used, in different coloured ink, though not for any apparent coding purpose. It appears, rather, that the writer added subsequent notes on revisiting the page or word in question.

The sources for Ó Foghludha's comments embrace numerous Irish poets, including those whose work he had edited.[56] Sources also include Geoffrey Keating, Aogán Ó Rathaille, Dáibhí Ó Bruadair, Molloy's 'Lucerna Fidelium', *An Grá agus an Ghruaim*, The Annals of Loch Cé, Kickham, and 'CCC'.[57] Placenemes are also given as sources — as previously mentioned, Ó Foghludha had published *A*

---

[55] Ibid.

[56] In his second letter to the Irish Texts Society in December 1935, he lists the fourteen volumes of eighteenth-century poetry from Munster edited by him, as well as *The Midnight Court*.

[57] The latter, which is cited very frequently, refers to Seán Óg Caomhánach's unpublished Irish-Irish Dictionary, *Croidhe Cainnte Ciarraighe*, although that abbreviation also occurs in Dinneen's list, referring to *Caithréim Conghail Cláiringnigh*. Ó Foghludha was appointed to edit *Croidhe Cainnte Ciarraighe* on behalf of the Department of Education, the intended publishers. Seán Óg commenced work on the dictionary in 1935 and finished in 1942. Ó Foghludha concluded his editing in 1943.

21

Dictionary of Irish Place-names in 1935 — and there are references to persons (such as Diarmuid Ó Mathghamhna, mentioned above) who seem to have been contemporary informants. In a note on the word 'maoineach', he gives his mother ('mo mháthair') as his source.

Some of the poets whose work is used as a reference are not well known but their work contained items that illustrated a usage that Ó Foghludha wished to highlight. For example, under the entry for 'súgha ... soot', Dinneen has 'cáibín súghaidh, a shabby hat (*S.W. Cork*)'. Ó Foghludha writes: 'This is wrong: <u>cáibín</u> here means a <u>cabin</u>; it also appears in poem by Diarmuid Mac Domhnaill Mic Fhinghin Chaoil'.[58] This work of this poet was also used to explain 'rian'; Dinneen translates 'rian' as 'a track, a path, a way ...' and Ó Foghludha adds 'Rian: condition, ability, circumstances, capacity', citing the example: 'cé fann mo rian' from a poem entitled 'An Brannda' by 'D.M.D.Mh.F.C'.[59]

Not every page is annotated but there are hardly ever more than three consecutive blank leaves. Some notes consist of a simple correction; for example: 'Fuarc ... chuir sé an scian go f. ionam; he stuck the knife in me to the very marrow' is corrected as '... to the <u>knife</u>'s own haft, <u>not</u> as printed'. On other occasions the correction is more disparaging of the editor, for example: 'Naoidhe ... in *phrase*: n. Dia isteach, a blessing used on entering a house; *similarly* n. Dia (is Muire) dhuit' which prompts the comment: 'This <u>naoidhe</u> marked opposite is surely very stupid in a Dictionary. In O'Growney booklets it is pointed out that this *naoidhe* is actually Go mbean[nuigh] Dia dhuit'. On another occasion, the comment is personal: 'Scríob ... cuirim fá scríb, I harrow (a field)'. Ó Foghludha declares:

---

[58] He does not give the example from the poem.

[59] Diarmuid mac Domhnaill mhic Fhinghin Chaoil Mhic Charrthaigh was an eighteenth-century Cork poet. The poem in question, 'An Brannda', can be found in J. O'Daly, *The Poets and Poetry of Munster: A Selection of Irish Songs by Poets of the last Century, with Poetical Translations by the late James Clarence Mangan* (Dublin and London, 1860) 282–4.

This is not the meaning I gave the editor 23 years ago for the first ed[ition]. *Cur fé fhód* means sowing corn by covering the seed by means of a plough. *Cur fé scríb* means covering the seed by means of the harrow, which is less satisfactory because the seed is not deep enough in the soil, but it is the readier method'.

'Marbh' elicits the following response: 'In the exp[lanation] "chomh marbh le h-Art" the meaning is not "as dead as <u>Art</u>" but rather "as dead as a STONE" (art = a stone — see p. 60, col. 2 of this book!)'. 'Art', as stated, occurs therein and is explained as 'a stone, a rock'. A further correction occurs on the same page: 'marbh-fhásc, a binding for the hands or feet of a corpse (marbh-fháisc ort, death take you)'; Ó Foghludha says: 'Marbh-fhásc (opp.) is not correctly explained. In Scots Gaelic it is conghlas, being a swathe or bandage used to hold up the human jaw after death'.

Dinneen's explanations of some of the uses of the noun 'mana' are minutely censured by Ó Foghludha who says: 'The meanings given here, generally, are incorrect or inexact. The word causes asp[iration], hence probably it unites as a compound in some instances at least'. According to Dinneen, '*m.deor* [means] an itching of the eyelid portending tears …'. According to Ó Foghludha, '*manadheor* is used as follows: "do mh–dh. nár chuirir díot" or "main do dheor nár chuirir díot". This is said of a person (particularly a child) who has been forcing himself to cry — out of stubborness. (blubbering)'. Dinneen explains that: '*m. creim cnámha* means "prurient itching or tendency"', but according to Ó Foghludha '*mana creidhm chnámh* means an itching of the <u>Jaws</u>, to be eating meat'. In the Dinneen version: '*m. póige* [means] an itching of the lip portending a kiss; mana póige nár chuirir díot, may your desire to kiss not be granted'. But, according Ó Foghludha, '*manaphóg* = somebody will be kissing [you] *cf.* "you'll be getting money" — when the palms tickle'. Ó Foghludha then adds: 'One meaning omitted opp[osite] is *mana chasta* = nostalgia, homesickness, a desire to return to the old nest; cf. "Tan ghlacfa mana chasta thú go lánghort Lugha, etc.", Séamus Mac Coitir'.

Dinneen's entry 'cómharaidheach, one who loans his labour ...' has been completely deleted by Ó Foghludha, who writes: 'not at all from *comhar* — cooperation. The 'r' is not broad, hence cóiridheach: the form cóiridhe (f) means in Corca Dhuibhne, a <u>funeral</u>. It does not seem to take medial <u>mh</u>. (See cóiridheach in *Additions and Corrections*)'. The entry in *Additions and Corrections* is 'coraidh' (for which the source is given as *B.C.C. — Betha Colaim Chille*): 'cóiridhe, funeral, and cómhairigheach (cóiridheach), funeral attender, are *prob.* to be referred to this word'.

Some of Ó Foghludha's additions are quite lengthy and in certain cases they include stanzas of poetry by way of illustration. For example, Dinneen explains 'cúbach' briefly as 'involute; having horns bent inwards; as *subs*[*stantive*], a cow with such horns ...'. Ó Foghludha adds at this point a list of 'other names for cows', although this is not relevant to the entry and he appears to have added an explanation of those names subsequently:

> ciúrach (gentle, mild), bléinfhionn (white / báinidhe), bricín (speckled), ceanann (geadach, white-faced or starred), ciardhubh (jet black), coilí, crónsach (swarthy, tall, copper coloured), deirgeach (reddy), donní (browny), druimfhionn (white backed), geadach, léithíneach, maoilín, réibhchín, scoithineach.[60]

In the following case, he not only provides lines of poetry to illustrate a word but also provides a local context for the lines. Under the entry 'sóirse', Dinneen refers us to 'séirse' and 'seoirse' but neither of these words corresponds to the explanation given by Ó Foghludha, which is:

> sóirse, a wisp (of hay, straw, etc.) *cf.* quatrain by Pádraig Phiarais Cúndún in Jimmy Hayes' hostelry in Killeagh: 'A chomhursna cad is dóigh libh don rígh

---

[60] The last items are followed by shorthand inscriptions.

úd thall / Ina stróinse i dtigh an ósta ina luighe go
fann, / Gan feoirling ina phóca do dhíolfadh ann / 'S
gan de choróin air act <u>sóirse</u> beag tuighe ar a cheann.[61]

Another such example is the word 'Údas'. Dineen's short
explanation is 'a Jew, a hard-hearted person'. Ó Foghludha
responds:

> This is surely very absurd — 'A Jew, a hard-hearted
> person!' Of course it is nothing more or less than
> <u>JUDAS</u>. And we have a well-known use of it by
> Piaras Mac Gearailt on the pervert Augustinian —
> John Power of Ballyhane, Co. Waterford: 'Ní sagart
> do bhí againn in intinn ná i dteagasc? Acht <u>Iúdas</u> do
> dhíolfadh ar fee beag, na Flaithis'.[62]

Finding Dinneen's version of 'loca' ('a sheepfold, a pen, a
pound, a lock [of wool, *etc.*]) inadequate, Ó Foghludha offers
three stanzas of poetry in order to illustrate the meaning of the
word. The poem in question, he says 'was composed by Rev.
Brian Mac Giolla Pádraig of Upper Ossory, grandson of the
Earl of Ossory. Brian was P.P. Durrow and V.G. of the Ossory
Diocese; he was seized in the time of Elizabeth in a cave in
that parish and put to death. No wonder we love them!'.[63]

Notes, in some cases, are superfluous to the entry in
question though no less interesting for that reason. For
example, Dinneen explains the adjective 'stadach' as
'stuttering; given to pausing, intermittent'. Ó Foghludha adds:
'*cf.* capall stadach = a jibbing horse: 4 miúile gan bheith
stadach / 4 gabhair gan bheith bradach / 4 ban gan bheith
cabach — sin dáréag ná fuil sa tír. *cf.* ceathrar sagart gan bheith

---

[61] 'Neighbours, what think ye of yonder king / a good-for-nothing stretched
prone in a hostelry / without a farthing in his pocket that he might spend there
/ and without a crown save a little wisp of straw on his head'.

[62] What we had was not a priest, in mind or in teaching? But a Judas who would
sell the Heavens for a small fee'.

[63] He had quoted two stanzas of the same poem to elaborate Dinneen's
translation of the word 'scairf'

sanntach etc., etc.'.[64] Sometimes, he adds a note explaining the derivation of a place-name related to the word in question; for example, 'Suaitreach'. Dinneen's version is: 'A Scandinavian warrior, a soldier, an officer ...'. Ó Foghludha adds: 'Suaitreach, Baile an tSuaitrigh, Ballintootra = Swatragh, Co. Derry'. Dinneen's gloss on the word 'philomeol' ('the nightingale') prompts a brief disquisition on the dubious claims for the existence of the bird in Ireland:

> the bird has never been proved to have visited Ireland: hence we don't appear to have a native word: the sedge warbler (?'plobóg na dtor') and the song-thrush have frequently been mistaken for her. The word 'smiolach' is probably for 'smólach', the song-thrush.[65] The Scots make only a trifling distinction — 'smólach' a thrush; 'smóltach' a nightingale, thrush. Kickham ['For the Old Land'] mentions 'the little bird' — night singer; and there were several mentions of it in *Dublin Penny Journal* over 100 years since. Kerry, Wexford, Cavan, Roscommon all claim to have heard the nightingale but the identity has not been proved.[66]

The leaves inserted in the last twelve pages of the Dictionary as well as those inserted thereafter in the section dealing with *Irregular Verbs and Additions and Corrections* are densely annotated; however, the notes do not relate to the adjacent items but, rather, seem to be random examples of usage, interspersed with shorthand inscriptions. These were probably added after the writer had completed his amendments to Dinneen's Dictionary. For example, the leaf facing p. 1297 is

---

[64] '4 mules that are not stubborn / 4 goats that do not trespass / 4 women that are not chatty — that's twelve that do not exist in the country. *cf.* four priests that are not avaricious, *etc., etc.*'.

[65] Vid. 'smíolach, *smiolach* / smíol, smiol: s. philomela, the thrush', in E. O'Reilly, *An Irish-English Dioctionary*, with a Supplement by John O'Donovan (Dublin, 1864). Seán Ó Coileáin referred me to this entry.

[66] Dinneen does not have an entry for 'plobóg na dtor'; he simply glosses 'plobóg' as 'a pollock, a chubby child'.

covered in notes, written in blue ink. These notes do not refer to any word on the facing page of the Dictionary apart from one item, written in a different ink: 'Ultan, Ultan, St. Ultan, cailín Ultain, a girl frequenting St. Ultan's pattern'. Ó Foghludha's note says 'Ultan: *cf.* Cathair Ultan, par[ish?] at Baile na <u>Martra</u> (= <u>relics</u>), Co. Cork'. A stanza inscribed on the first inserted leaf of the second volume is not related to any entry; the stanza in question is the envoy (ceangal), found in some versions of Liam Inglis's poem 'An tAodhaire Óg'.[67] This poem, without the envoy, is included in Ó Foghludha's *Cois na Bríde*.[68]

As these examples demonstrate, Ó Foghludha's amendments and additions draw on diverse sources, both written and oral and are not confined to one dialect region.

Seán Óg Caomhánach and his Copy of the Dictionary

Seán Óg Caomhánach, known as 'Seán an Chóta', was born in Clochar, in the West Kerry Gaeltacht, in 1885 and grew up in nearby Dunquin. When he was eighteen, he was appointed to the post of travelling teacher of Irish in Fermoy, and eight years later, he moved to Dublin, where he wrote for Arthur Griffith's paper, *Sinn Féin*, under the pseudonym 'Catharach Nua'. In 1914, he emigrated to America, remaining there until 1922, and his novel *Fánaí* is based on his experiences during those years. On returning to Ireland, he took the Republican side in the Civil War and was incarcerated in Tintown in the Curragh for a year after which he worked as an Irish teacher in Dublin. In 1935, the Department of Education invited him to compile an Irish-Irish dictionary, based on local words from his native Corca Dhuibhne, asking that he make a special effort to seek out words that were not included in Dinneen's Dictionary. The result of this research, *Croidhe Cainnte Ciarraighe*, which amounts to twenty-nine volumes and over two million words, was never published but the manuscript is held in the National Library of Ireland (MS G 601–29). An

---

[67] See Ú. Nic Éinrí, *Canfar an Dán* (An Daingean, 2003) 237.
[68] (Baile Átha Cliath, 1937) 24–5.

inscription at the end of G 629 reads: 'Ar n-a chríochnughadh ar an 30adh lá d'Easbafuilt, 1942 a bhuidhe le Dia. Seán an Chóta' ('Concluded on the 30th day of November, 1942, thanks be to God. Seán an Chóta'). This is followed by the inscription 'Críoch don eagar fám láimhse 11.v.1943; 9.20p.m. A bhuidhe le Dia — amen. Risteárd Ó Foghludha'. ('Concluding the editorship at my hand 11.v.1943; 9.20p.m. Thanks be to God — amen. Risteárd Ó Foghludha'). Seán Óg Caomhánach died in 1947.[69]

Seán Óg's two-part interleaved copy of the 1927 edition of Dinneen's Dictionary is divided at the word 'lusradh' (p. 688) but in this case the notes have been provided not just by one person, Seán an Chóta, but also by his brother, Séamus Caomhánach. Séamus was born in 1900 and, having qualified as a primary teacher in 1924, he was awarded a B.A. five years later and, in 1930 he went to study at the University of Bonn. In 1931, he completed an M.A. dissertation on 'The Vocabulary of the West-Kerry Dialect of Irish'.[70] In the Foreword, he writes:

> The words edited here have been gathered mostly in the parish of Dún Chaoin in West Kerry. Comparisons have been made between those words in forms, usages etc. and as they are found in Dinneen's Irish-English Dictionary [1927]. New words have been recorded, and additional usages have been given in cases where it seemed worth doing so. I have not so far as I know, unnecessarily repeated anything contained in that book.

Séamus was appointed Professor of Celtic Languages and Philology at University College Cork in 1946 and held that post until 1970. He died in 1989.

---

[69] S. Ó Lúing, *Seán an Chóta* (Baile Átha Cliath, 1985) 7–25 *et passim*. See also, N. Ó Brosnacháin, *Éist leis an gCóta* (Maigh Nuad, 2001).

[70] I am grateful to Seán Ó Coileáin who made a copy of this dissertation available to me.

The personal bitterness that was apparent in Ó Foghludha's comments is absent from the notes in Seán an Chóta's copy of the Dictionary and these notes tend to be briefer than Ó Foghludha's. Seán's notes, in particular, consist mainly of a simple gloss on Dinneen's word.[71] Given that both Seán and Séamus Caomhánach had already produced extensive lists of words (and usages) that were *not* in the 1927 edition of Dinneen's Dictionary, it seems extraordinary that they were still able to produce additional material based on a further examination of that Dictionary. Probably for that reason, the notes in their copy are less dense than those in Ó Foghludha's.

Seán Óg's *Croidhe Cainnte Ciarraighe*

Seán Óg does not refer to Dinneen in *CCC*; he simply gives a word, followed by meanings and usages as Dinneen does in his Dictionary.[72] And, while his brief from the Department of Education was that he seek out words that were not in Dinneen's Dictionary, his lists are not just based on such words but on words that *are* in Dinneen and to which he adds supplementary meanings or usages. For example:

bábánta:
Dinneen: *indec*[*linable*] *a.*, childish, innocent.
Seán Óg: *a.* cúthail, maol, ciúin. Nách bábánta an duine é ná druidfeadh isteach: nách cúthail, neamh-dhána é. Ná bí chomh <u>bábánta</u> san: chomh neamh-chainnteach san, abair rud éigin.

ciabhach:
Dinneen: *a.*, hairy, bushy, having long hair; dishevelled, unkempt.
Seán Óg: *a.* gruaigeach, fadfholtach, mothalach-gliobach, foltscaoilte. Dá bhfeaca riamh ní fheaca bean budh <u>chiabhaighe</u> 'ná í, ar chaol a droma

---

[71] It is possible to recognise which of the brothers is responsible for the note in question because Seán uses the old Irish script whereas Séamus uses the Roman script.

[72] Dinneen's comments are in English, Seán Óg's in Irish.

stadadh a folt: budh shia gruaig 'ná í. Daoine ciabhacha seadh na Rúisigh: daoine mothalacha: muirearghruaigeach: gruaig fhada throm ar gach aoinne aca. B'annamh leat bheith chomh ciabhacha 's ataoi, bíonn an ghruaig cíortha sleamhain ort de ghnáth: gan í bheith triopalach, gasta, réidh. Bíonn búndúinín ciabhach bán ar an gcoinín: lóca beag bán ar árd a thóna. Ainmhidhe ciabhach seadh madra: fionna fada air.

leibéis:
Dinneen: *f.*, carelessness, unconcern, clumsiness.
Seán Óg: (libéis) *b.*2. neamhchríochnamhlacht, faillighe, neamhaire, fuairthéacht, neamhshuim, manaois, liobarnacht. Sin é, tuiteadh a's briseadh gach aon rud as do lámhaibh, ní leigfeadh an leibéis duit é: liobarnacht. Diúltuighimís do ach is dócha gur b'é an leibéis a fhág amuigh é, fairír: ceal aire cheart budh bhun lé n-a bhás. Ní le ceal eólais ná deineann sé obair seacht n-uaire níos fearr ach le leibéis: neamhchúramacht a's neamhshuim. Leis an leibéis, Dia linn, tá a chlann gan luid den éadach ortha ná leath a ndóthain lé n-itheadh: fuairthéacht .i. is cuma leis ceaca: choidhche ní buailtear 'n-a aigne go bhfuilid 'n-a ngábhtar.

toirtín:
Dinneen: *m.*, a small mass or quantity, a cake, a loaf; a dwarf; toirtín reisíní, a fruit cake; toirtín bog, a sponge cake; toirtín lóin, bread for a journey; toirtín neoinín, a cake of oatmeal and new milk baked between two cabbage leaves under the embers, toirtín fa luaith, *prob.id.*, subcinericium panem (*Kea*[*ting*]); toirtín céireach, a small cake of wax.

Seán Óg: *f* 4. ádhbhairín, téagar beag, méidín, cáca, bullóg. Toirtín bog: cáca bog eadtrom milis déanta de phlúr, de shiúicre is d'uibhibh. Toirtín rísínidhe: déanta lé rísíndhibh ann. An toirtín atá aige ní thógfainn in ao'chor é, aithis é do tharrac (tairgsint) do dhuine an bheag-mhéid. Fair an chaora is bíodh an toirtín agat: an té (go mór-mór ógánach) a gheobhadh uan nó laogh nuadh-bheartha gheibheadh sé cáca as, níl deireannaighe anuas uibhe. Gach maidean is é ag gluaiseacht chun bóthair bhuaileadh sé chuige toirtín lóin: arán i gcóir a aistir.

Séamus Caomhanach's 'The Vocabulary of the West-Kerry Dialect of Irish'

While Dinneen is not his only point of reference in his thesis, 'The Vocabulary of the West-Kerry Dialect of Irish' (*DWK*), Séamus Caomhánach refers to that source in the great majority of the items he lists — either because the word in question is *not* in Dinneen, or because it is and he is offering additional usages. For example:

> 'báinté', *f. not* in Din; a dead calm; tá an fhairrge na báinté, the sea is very calm; ta an lá 'na bainte, the day is very calm; also bánté' and he gives as his source, AH (*Allagar na hInise*, page and line).

> 'brabúsach', adj., *not* in Din., seeking unfair advantage of another; covetous; duine brabúsach e sin …, he is a person who seeks unfair advantage over his fellow. Dinneen gives both 'brabús' and 'brabúsaidhe' (nouns) but not the adjective.

> 'boghaisín', *m. as* in Din. Also, ag déanamh boghaisíní, approaching anything discreetly and indirectly; bhí sé ag déanamh boghaisíní timcheall Sheáin, i dtaobh an chleamhnais, he was trying to negotiate diplomatically with Seán about the marriage.

31

Seán and Séamus Caomhánach's Notes and Additions: Some Examples

Seán Óg's notes in the interleaved volumes of Dinneen are generally brief, offering an extra usage or simply a variant of the expression, following the same system he used in *CCC*. For example: Dinneen explains 'spiacaidheacht' as 'a fondness for brilliancy of colour, *etc.*; an fhaid is beo í an bhean mairfidh an spiacaidheacht innte, while woman lives her fondness for bright colours will live'. Seán Óg adds: '1) an fhaid is beo bean mairfidh an spiagaidheacht ina fuil: an taithneamh do dhathannaibh'.

Dinneen's entry for 'sclábhaidhe' is 'a serf or slave, a workman, a day labourer, an agricultural drudge: is tu an sclábhaidhe, what a wretch you are (*Don.*)'. Seán Óg adds: 'ní hé an sclábhaidhe is fearr is mó rath'.

One noun that elicited a very substantial response from Seán Óg, however, is 'bean'. In this instance, he elaborates on Dinneen's already substantial entry by offering thirty (numbered) expressions generally pertaining to 'woman / women / wife'. The list of expressions — many of which would be considered unacceptable today on the grounds of political correctness — is as follows:

1) bean geal [sic] dubh an bhean is breághtha amuigh.
2) bean dubh ar tosach an uilc; bean bán [sic] ar tosach na ngrást; bean ruadh ar tosach an tsluaigh. 3) is fearr bean bheag deas ná bean mhór gránda. 4) bean nó muc ist oidhche. 4) [the previous number again, in error?] bean gan aprún nó bó gan earball [taibhbhrighid neamhshlachtmhar]. 5) is leath beathaidh bean mhaith tighe. 6) ní daoi go mnaoi droich-mhéine. 7) bíonn múineadh ar fhear ó aois go bás ach ní bhíonn múineadh ar mhnaoi go lá an bhráth [sic]. 8) iarr ar mhnaoi é uair nó dhó agus mara dtagaid leat tair leo. 9) cara mná tighe [is maith í do bheith ar thaobh duine]. 10) ná bac aoinne ná bíonn buidheachas na mban air. 11) an fad is beo an bhean mairfidh an spiagaidheacht 'na súil. (This example

was also given by Dinneen — quoted above — under his entry for 'spiacaidheacht'). 12) tabhair do ghrádh dod mhnaoi agus do rún dod mháthair. 13) is fearr briathra dána diana do mhnaoi ná í bheith ciallmhar riaghalta mánla mín. 14) is fearr dul ag fiafraighe na trágha na dul ag fiafraighe droch-mhná. 15) is measa na mná ná an t-ól. 16) is deacair taobh do thabhairt leis na mnáibh. 17) ní dheaghaidh aoinne riamh amach ar intinn mná. 18) tar éis na mionn is fearr na mná. 19) smachtuigheann gach aoinne an bhean mhínáireach ach an té go mbíonn sí aige. 20) is dána bean ná muc agus is dána muc ná an diabhal. 21) fead glaice ag mnaoi cearc ag glaodhach. 22) cearc bán [sic] ar chearcaibh nó file mná i mbaile. 23) beirt [scata] bhan nó scata géadhanna. 24) díothughadh a cine bean bheag gránda.[73] 25) bean óg gan náire nó gáire gan éifeacht. 26) fallaidhe fuara do ghní óinseacha. 27) fallaidhe fuara do ghní bean tighe guagach. 28) is fearr éagconn caillighe ná éagconn cailín. 29) an chailleach is sine is í is mine. 29) [the previous number again, in error?] arm caillighe cloch. 30) ní fhéuchfadh bean siar chun leathscéil d'fháil.

And he adds: 'ní ólann na mná puinn ach imigheann an deoch mar a mbíd'. Séamus adds 'bean nó anairt ní féidir breith a thabhairt orthu istoidhche'.

Dinneen's entry for the noun 'fear' — which is over twice as long as his entry for 'bean' — elicits a further list of related expressions from Seán Óg which, again, he numbers:

1) is mairg tigh ná taithighid fir. 2) is sirriam teallaigh gach fear ar a thinteán fein. 3) is minic do thuit fear maith i gcac bó (bualtach). 4) ní raibh cuibheasach ina thigheasach mhaith riamh. 5) fear óg díomhaoin adhbar an tseanduine bhuain. 6) is minic a bhí fear

---

[73] Opposite Dinneen's 'díothughadh', Séamus has inserted the same expression though, apparently with a misprint: 'díothughadh a cine beag [sic] bheag ghránna'.

maith i seanbhríste. 7) ní fear é ar aonach ná ar mhargadh ná ar phobal an Aifrinn. 8) ní hiad na fir fhada (mhóra) a bhaineas an fóghmhar. 9) is fearr feairín ar fhearaibh ná fear ar fheairínibh. 10) fear beag ar árdán nó fear mór ar ísleán = comhthrom. 11) níl laoch dá throime ná faightear fear a chloídh. 12) deireadh fir a shuan; deireadh mná á faire féin fuar. 13) is fearr lán duirn d'fhear ná lán gaid de mhnaoi.

Apart from the last two contributions, Séamus's notes are generally more comprehensive than Seán Óg's, consisting of further additional usages, sometimes with, sometimes without an explanation in English. For example, '"anaiteas", *m.* according to Dinneen means: ill-humour, anger; festering; pain, discomfort, foulness of weather; ag déanamh anaitis damh, troubling me'. On the facing leaf, Séamus has added: '1) Tá sé dulta chun *anaitis* leis an ól (= olc ar fad); 2) Téarnóigh an teine nó raghaidh sí chun anaitis (lasfaidh sí nó raghaidh sí chun deire); 3) Tá an lá dulta chun anaitis'. Again:

> 'caoch', according to Dinneen means: blind, dim-eyed, dim, closed-up, blasted (as wheat, nuts *etc.*); fear dall, a blind man; fear caoch, a dim-, one- or squint-eyed man, a blindman (*abusive*); neanntóg, a variety of nettles; cnó caoch, a blind nut; cnó caoch i ná bíonn amhmhaoin, a blind nut without substance; tobar caoch, a disused or dry well; an taobh caoch díom, my blind or unguarded side; completely 'blind', deceived, confused, subdued, as by hunger *etc.*; (go) caoch, completely; bhuail sé caoch sramach é, he beat him black and blue (with words or blows); defective in speech (*Meath*); leath-chaoch, blind of an eye.

On the facing leaf, Séamus has added:

> 1) chó caoc [sic] le circ. 2) gura caoiche amáireach tu. 3) nách caoch a eirigh se dho. 4) solas caoch atá ón lampa san. 5) cró caoch atá sa tsnáthaid sin. 6) caoch go rabhair a amadáin. 7) níl inti ach bearna chaoch (ro

34

chumhaing). **8**) díol prátaí go mbíonnsúile caocha iontu ní maith iad. **9**) simné caoch ar thig. **10**) dath caoch iseadh an dath san. **11**) tháinig sé ar an dtaobh caoch do (dhein sé bob a bhuala air). **12**) bhí sé caoch glan ar meisce. **13**) giorrfhiadh caoch go mbéarfadh an chú san air.

In the case of certain words, Séamus has added a numerical reference (or in some cases, a series of references). These references, which are in red ink, appear to have been added at a later date. They do not give a word or a meaning but refer to a usage in the context of the source referred to, although the source is not identified. One such example, 'críoch' has ten sets of numbers appended and all but one correspond to a page and line number in Tomás Criomhthain's *An tOileánach* (An Seabhac's 1929 edition) where the word in question occurs:[74]

> **80,12** ('Sé <u>críoch</u> agus deire na mbeart é gur ghaibh an deoch lastuas ar fad an lá san de'. **106.7** (?) **111,16** ('… agus is minic adeireadh sé ná raibh aon <u>chríoch</u> riamh ar an té do bheadh ar shlait a dhroma sa leabhaidh agus an ghrian go soillseach ar an spéir, agus fós gur dhroich-ní dho'n tsláinte é'). **180,3** ('Sé <u>críoch</u> agus deire an scéil é go raibh an lá nach mór meilte againn ag féachaint ar so súd san am gur bhaineamair amach cé na Coise'). **183,2** ('… gurbh é <u>críoch</u> agus deire na mbeart é gurbh' fhuirist é chóimhreamh gach ar dhíolamair de chíos riamh ó shin'). **187,21** ('Sin <u>críoch</u> leis an mbeirt do chuir sioladh na teangan so im' chluasa an chéad lá'). **189,2** ('Sé <u>críoch</u> agus deire na mbeart é nár chuir aenne de'n mbeirt a thuairisc riamh ó shin'). **200,18** ('Dob é <u>críoch</u> agus deire na mbeart é go raibh sé geal a dhóthain san am gur bhogamair agus dob' 'in é an uair díreach a tháinig an conach ar lucht na n-amhrán'). **214,26** ('Ní raibh <u>críoch</u> ná áird ar an méid a bhí

---

[74] *An t-Oileánach: Scéal a Bheathadh Féin, do scríobh Tomás Ó Criomhthain*, An Seabhac do chuir i n-eagar (Baile Átha Cliath, 1929).

curtha aige féin, mar fear bocht aonair dob' eadh é agus do bhíodh a thurus ins gach áit agus fágann an turusóireacht breall go minic ar ghnóthaí eile'). **234,3** ('Seadh, do bhí <u>críoch</u> curtha ar mhuca min na déirce agus ar na banbhaí a deineadh a cheannach aon lá amháin ar mhargadh Dhaingin Uí Chúise').[75]

Dinneen does not distinguish between 'críoch' and 'crích' but Séamus adds a further series of numbers showing examples of the latter, where the two forms have diverged slightly in meaning, all examples from the same edition of *An tOileánach*:

29,29 ('Sin an <u>chrích</u> a chuaidh ar an gcéad mhúinteoir scoile a tháinig go dtí an Bloscaod'). **135,16** ('criú an bháid againn-ne imithe gan <u>chrích</u> san am san'). **137,5,7** ('A' bhfuil aon <u>chrích</u> fós ort ach mar fhágas cheana thu?' 'Nach maith a' <u>chrích</u> an bolg a bheith lán'). **164,4** ('Sin é <u>crích</u> d'imigh ar mo chlainn-se'). **195,24** ('Fé mar dubhart cheana do bhí orm a bheith im' bhuachaill aige i n-ionad a bheith im' mháighistir nó ní bheadh <u>crích</u> orainn'). **260,24** ('Do bhíos annsan gan aon duine chun aon <u>chrích</u> a chur orm, ach sinn go breallach ag tarrac an tsaoghail 'nár ndiaidh'). And, he gives an example in the genitive: **228,32** ('Ní mí-bhuidheach do bhíos féin d'fhear an tighe mar gheall ar an méid sin <u>críche</u> chur orm mar do bhíos ré-shuaithte toisc me bheith laethannta óm' thigh féin agus óm' baile dúthchais').

Dinneen includes examples of crích, but as a dative of 'críoch', not as a separate noun: 'Cia hí an cailín a bheadh gan chrích? What girl would remain unmarried? Ag imeacht gan chrích, going for naught; cuirim cailín i gcrích, I get a daughter married; tagaim i gcrích, I am fulfilled, come to pass'.

On the same leaf as that which contains his numerical references, Séamus has added a further note, without any

---

[75] The one page and line reference where the word does not occur (**106,7**) may simply be an error.

reference to *An tOileánach*, and using the noun in the dative as Dinneen does in his examples: 'chuir sé an cailín ó chrích (leanbh a bheith aige léithe agus gan í phósadh)'.

'Críoch' does not occur in *DWK* but Seán Óg has a long entry in *CCC*, where he gives both forms as variants of the same noun: '"críoch, b2 (crích)" deireadh, teora, cosc, imeall; ceann scríbe; rún; sochrughadh cinnte; sochrughadh pósta; toradh; dúthaigh; cóiriughadh; iomartas; meabhrughadh aon ruda; taisce'. Among the examples of usage that he gives are: 'B'é <u>crích</u> na mbeart nár réidhtigheadar le chéile: b'é deireadh a n-imtheachta. ... Clann óg atá i bhfad ó <u>chrích</u> iad: i bhfad ó bheith i ndán aon rud tairbheach do dhéanamh lé n-a laige'. In the interleaved Dinneen, as a further elaboration of the noun 'críoch', Seán Óg explains the verb 'críochnuighim' as follows: 'chríochnuigh sé an dúthaigh: dhein sé a roinnt agus léirscáil do dhéanamh di'.

Séamus provides fifteen numerical references to exemplify the use of Dinneen's entry 'ionbhaidh': 'time or hour, a particular, approximate or predetermined time; the time of parturition; season, as of fruit, *etc.*'; he gives 'ionbhadh' as an alternative form. All of Séamus's references are to *An tOileánach* and the examples identified by him all demonstrate the same usage, for example: **24,28**: 'B'shin ionbhadh ag an Rí é'; **79,10,26**: 'dob 'in ionbhadh age Paidí é'; **207,18**: 'dob 'in ionbhadh agam-sa é'; **238,3**: 'do b'in ionbhadh agam-sa, leis, é'. None of the examples contained in Dinneen's entry show this usage. They include: 'as ionbhaidh, out of season; tar ionbhaidh, having its season passed, beyond due time; tá an ionbhaidh agam, I have the opportunity; sul dá raibh sé d'ionbhaidh aige, ere he had time; glac t'ionbhaidh, take your time (*Con.*); an ionbhaidh sin, at that time'. Seán Óg has added a note also: 'Tá an traen in ionbhaidh ach níl sí anso fós'.

Regarding Séamus's references to 'ionbhadh' in An Seabhac's edition of *An tOileánach*, Seán Ó Coileáin comments as follows:

> In fact it is most unlikely that *ionbhadh*, the reading of An Seabhac's edition of *An tOileánach*, which sparked the interest of Séamus in this much-discussed

phrase, has anything to do with *ionbhaidh* (Old Irish *inbaid*), pronounced *ionú* in the spoken language of West Kerry,[76] or indeed with anything else. Nor is a form *ionbhadh* supported by by the manuscript readings of *An tOileánach* which it is intended to represent. In the examples quoted above the author, Tomás Ó Criomhthain, writes: *Bin nua ag an rí é; do bin nua aige Paidí é; do bin nua agamsa leis é*. The most recent editor has adopted the suggestion of Máire Mhac an tSaoi that *nua* should be understood as *nó* in such locutions.[77] This *ionbhadh* can safely be dismissed as a ghost word invented by An Seabhac in an effort to explain the meaning of the idiom.

It would seem, therefore, that Séamus's numerical references reflect on the misunderstanding of An Seabhac rather than any inaccuracy on the part of Dinneen (apart from his note that 'ionbhadh' is an alternative form of 'ionbhaidh').

The word 'fearthain', glossed by Dinneen as 'act of raining; rain; tá sé ag cur fearthana, it is raining' is followed by a note by Seán Óg: 'fearthain a chiúnuigheann gaoth; fearthain a scaipeas ceo' and this note is followed by four numerical references by Séamus, all to *An tOileánach*. The examples, in this case, do not appear to enhance Dinneen's explanation of the word. 'Gomh' does not occur in Dinneen but on the leaf facing p. 561 Séamus has written: 'gomh' with four references to the word as it occurs in *An tOileánach*. 'Seift' and 'seanntán' are similarly noted.

An tOileánach is referenced where Dinneen is perceived as being incorrect, as in the case of the entry 'cigire'. Dinneen writes: 'an inspector (a spurious word now in common use)'. Opposite this, Séamus has given seven numerical references, all of which occur within two pages of Ó Criomhthain's book and refer to the same incident. Dinneen's description of the word as 'spurious' could be defended in this case as the use of the word by Ó Criomhthain is confined to the

---

[76] Dinneen adds: '*pron[ounced]* ionúig (M[unster]), ionú (Con[naught])'.
[77] S. Ó Coileáin (eag.), *An tOileánach* (Baile Átha Cliath, 2002) p. xxxiv.

incident described and involved a concept that was not part of his traditional narrative.

However, not all of the numbers in red refer to Ó Criomhthain's book. *Lá dár Saol* by Tomás's son, Seán, is referenced also:[78] "'Cé hiad so?" adúrt. "Táthar ann," arsa Bod ... Lá p. 120'. **255, 27** on the same page refers to (but does not name) *An tOileánach* where we read: 'is le grean atáid siad tógtha agus táthán tríd'. The word 'táthán', 'cement, is not in Dinneen but the reference is probably to the entry 'táthadh: act of welding, soldering joining: iad do tháthadh le chéile, to weld them, to wed them'. I was unable to identify the source of all of the numerical references, having excluded *An tOileánach*, *Lá dar Saol* and *Allagar na hInise*.

The examples chosen above are representative rather than comprehensive. A thorough analysis of *CCC* or *DWK* or of Dinneen's Larger Dictionary is beyond the scope of this booklet.

Conclusion

Although Risteárd Ó Foghludha's volumes, with their amendments and additions, were purchased by the Irish Texts Society on the understanding that they would be incorporated into a Supplement of the Dictionary, this had not been part of the original plan. When Dinneen was consulted, shortly before his death about his views on a possible Supplement, he had emphasised the need to include 'material which has appeared in print since the book was published'; many of Ó Foghludha's notes do not fall within that category. Séamus Caomhánach's references to *An tOileánach* would do so, but only in the literal sense of the word, as the manuscript from which the book was edited predated the publication of the Dictionary. The comments and amendments in the case of both Ó Foghludha and the Caomhánach brothers do not appear to have been written for an independent reader.[79] How the two sets of half-volumes came to be in the possession of their respective

---

[78] S. Ó Criomhthain, *Lá dár Saol* (Baile Átha Cliath, 1969).

[79] The fact that many of Séamus Caomhánach's numerical references are not immediately identifiable supports this opinion.

owners is not known either. How they came to be at the disposition of this writer can be explained, however.

Afterword

In 2011, I was presented with the first half-volume of Ó Foghludha's interleaved copy of Dinneen by my friend, Tomás Ó Briain, scholar and bibliophile, who had discovered it in a Charity shop. To my great surprise, I was made aware shortly afterwards that what appeared to be the second half-volume was for sale at an upcoming antiquarian book auction. I duly arranged to purchase it. I had been discussing this fortunate discovery with my colleague, Professsor Seán Ó Coileáin, who informed me that he had in his possession a similar pair of annotated half-volumes, which had been given to him by the late Professor Séamus Caomhánach and he kindly offered to lend me the pair. I wanted to ensure that such a unique source of the language and such a valuable addition to the monumental opus that is Dinneen's Dictionary should not remain concealed and forgotten but should be brought to the attention of an interested public. Seán Ó Coileáin and I decided that once I had completed my short survey of their contents, the two sets of half-volumes should be presented to the Archives of the Irish Texts Society in the Special Collections Department of the Boole Library, University College Cork, where they will be permanently available for consultation.

I would like to express my gratitude to Tomás Ó Briain for his inspiring gift and to Seán Ó Coileáin for his support and for his many helpful comments on this text. I would also like to acknowledge Kevin Murray's editorial expertise.

Printed in Great Britain
by Amazon

67602608R00031